LEARN AMERICAN
SIGN LANGUAGE

EVERYTHING YOU NEED TO START SIGNING

COMPLETE BEGINNER'S GUIDE • 800+ SIGNS

JAMES W. GUIDO

WELLFLEET
PRESS

Brimming with creative inspiration, how-to projects, and useful information to enrich your everyday life, Quarto Knows is a favorite destination for those pursuing their interests and passions. Visit our site and dig deeper with our books into your area of interest: Quarto Creates, Quarto Cooks, Quarto Homes, Quarto Lives, Quarto Drives, Quarto Explores, Quarto Gifts, or Quarto Kids.

First published in 2015 by Wellfleet Press,
an imprint of The Quarto Group,
142 West 36th Street, 4th Floor
New York, NY 10018, USA
T (212) 779-4972 F (212) 779-6058
www.QuartoKnows.com

Wellfleet titles are also available at discount for retail, wholesale, promotional, and bulk purchase. For details, contact the Special Sales Manager by email at special-sales@quarto.com or by mail at The Quarto Group, Attn: Special Sales Manager, 100 Cummings Center Suite 265D, Beverly, MA 01915 USA.

15

ISBN-13: 978-1-57715-107-4

A Green Tiger Book
www.greentigerbooks.com

Photography by Mark A. Gore
Cover and interior design by Lynne Yeamans
Photography Assistant: Daniel Stasser
Models: Shelly Guy and Garret Zuercher

Printed in China

>> CONTENTS

>> INTRODUCTION

Welcome to the world of American Sign Language (ASL)! ASL is a vibrant, easy-to-learn language that is used by approximately half a million people each day. This book will lead you through everything you need to know to have a basic knowledge of ASL, including the basics of signing (including handshapes, palm orientation, location, movement, and facial expressions), grammar and sentence structure, and some helpful tips for learning ASL.

The first thing you should know about ASL and its language is that ASL is not English! Even though English speakers and users of ASL utilize the same written language, spoken English and ASL are quite different from each other. ASL has a separate foundation than spoken (or written) English, and its users have different needs. We ASL speakers not only have our own grammar and structure rules, we have unique and different ways of expressing ourselves. The more you learn about ASL and Deaf culture, the more you will come to understand the way Deaf people communicate! This introduction will give you a good place to start.

THE BASICS OF SIGNING

First thing's first: "Which hand should I use?" is a common question for a new learner of ASL. However, it's really as simple as using whatever hand you're most comfortable with. (That way, your signing won't look "stiff.") This hand is referred to as your "dominate hand" throughout the book. You should also use your dominate hand for finger-spelling (spelling out words you don't know the sign for or that have no sign).

Before you jump right into learning words in ASL, it's important to understand a few of the fundamentals of the language, so you can be sure to sign correctly. Signs have five different aspects you should know about, called the five main parameters of ASL: Handshape, Palm Orientation, Location, Movement, and Facial Expression.

HANDSHAPES

ASL has a variety of handshapes that are used to create signs or classify them (see below). These handshapes may be actual shapes (for instance, holding your hands like whiskers when making the sign for "Cat"), or the letter of the alphabet that that sign begins with (for instance, "Fruit" is signed using the handshape "F"). Learning the manual alphabet

CAT >> Make your hands look like whiskers when signing "Cat."

FRUIT >> Many signs, like "Fruit," are formed with a handshape in the letter of the alphabet they begin with.

(pages 12–15) is a great place to start when learning ASL–both because the alphabet is used in so many signs, and because you can "finger spell" words you don't know.

Classifiers

Classifiers are handshapes and movements that describe size, shape, weight, action, and/or quantity in ASL. By using classifiers, a gift you received quickly and easily becomes a giant, heavy gift you received, and a story about walking down the street can instantly be transformed into a story about two people walking down the street, simply by modifying the sign. In proper ASL grammar, a classifier is used after you sign the main sign.

Although I've tried to give you lots of examples of classifiers you can use for various words throughout this book, the sky's the limit when it comes to classifiers. Basically, there's no rule saying what handshape you can't use, as long as you indicate the right size, shape, direction

of movement, and/or location. (Just remember to sign the original word first!) Therefore, it's important to practice your ASL signs using a variety of handshapes, so that you can be comfortable using them to modify your signs.

PALM ORIENTATION

The second parameter of a sign is your palm orientation–which way your palm is facing. It's important to note the orientation of your palm because different palm directions can have drastically different meanings! For instance, "Year" and "Bar mitzvah" are signed using a similar movement, but the palms are facing in different directions.

LOCATION

Location is exactly what it sounds like–where you sign. While signing, you have to make sure you're signing in the right location. For instance, to sign "Summer," you move an "X" handshape across your forehead. To sign

YEAR

BAR/BAT MITZVAH

>> The signs for "Year" and "Bar mitzvah" are similar except for the palm orientation.

"Ugly," you make the same handshape and movement, except you do it under your nose instead. You wouldn't want to confuse summer and ugliness!

MOVEMENT

As you've already seen, ASL is a 3-D, visual language, so it's no surprise movement is an essential part of signing. The movement of your hands can indicate a direction, location, or who you're referring to. It's similar to Location, but is usually used to describe action. For example, when you're signing "Nice to meet you!" (page 34), sign "Meet" toward yourself away from the person you're meeting. Similarly, the only difference between "I showed it to you" and "I showed it to her" is signing the word "Show" in the direction of the person you showed.

You can fuse together more than one movement to make a compound sign. For instance, if you're telling a story where you opened a door and then closed it, you can simply make the sign for "Door" (page 70) then make the motion of opening and closing it with your hand. In this way, ASL can be tremendously more efficient than spoken English—oftentimes the words to convey actions take much longer than motions!

FACIAL EXPRESSIONS

Facial expressions may be the most important parameter of ASL. Since users of ASL aren't required to use our voices, we use our faces to express meaning and emphasis. Remember, ASL *is* your voice! In the same way that you would emphasize certain words, pause for effect, or use your voice to tell a story in spoken English, make sure to do the same when signing with ASL by using your face. The people who you're communicating with will be relying on your face to help them understand the meaning of what you're signing! There many different ways you can use your face to relay meaning:

Emotions

Just as saying the same word in a different way can completely change your meaning, the expression of emotion on your face can completely change the meaning of what you're signing. For instance, the facial expression for the word "Stole" would be completely different if you were saying, "My shoes were stolen" versus, "I stole my sister's French fries." I've tried to help you out throughout the book by reminding you to emphasize your facial expression on signs were it's particularly important.

Eyebrows and Head Movements

When asking questions in ASL, it's important to use your eyebrows to indicate a questioning look. The lack of this facial expression can change a question into a statement: For instance, "Are you Deaf?" is "You are Deaf" without a questioning face! You can practice this look by simply asking a puzzling question out loud, and noting the shape your face makes: Your eyebrows will pinch together, and your head may even tilt.

There's another way eyebrow and head movements are used while signing. Raised eyebrows and/or a slight nod are often used when mentioning the topic of a sentence. For instance, if I was telling someone how much I like ice cream, when making the sign for "Ice Cream" (page 138) I would raise my eyebrows and nod a bit. (Then, of course, when I made the sign for "Like," my facial expression would show how much I like it!)

Non-Manual Signals

Also called NMS or "Manuals," these signals are formed by your lips and other facial expressions, and are usually used as adjectives to modify other signs to describe their size, shape, weight, and/or motion. For instance, to indicate a large house, sign "House" (page 68) using a "Puff" or "Cha" facial expression; if you're talking about a small house, sign "House" while making an "Ooo" expression. Non-manual signs can also be used to indicate intensity, for example, to indicate that you've been studying hard, sign "Study" (page 116) while making the "Puff" expression; to sign that studying has been just an average amount of work, sign "Study" while making the "Mmm" expression (and sign less furiously). You'll notice that the "Puff" expression is one you might make anyway when talking about preparing for a hard test—this is another way using ASL

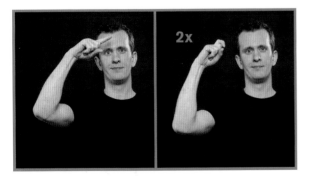

SUMMER

UGLY

>> The signs for "Summer" and "Ugly" are similar, except for their location.

can be much more efficient than the spoken word. There's no need to communicate "it's been hard" when it's showing all over your face! In addition to reminders to make sure to use your facial expressions to their best advantage, you'll also find references to specific non-manual signals throughout the book. They include:

OOO >> Used to express few in number, or something that is small, thin, or light.

MMM >> Used for several, medium, or average.

CHA >> Made when there is a lot of something, or to express largeness or heaviness.

PUFF >> Similar to "Cha," is used to express largeness in quantity or size.

SOA >> Soa is used to indicate high intensity, such as working hard.

SSS >> Sss is used to indicate closeness in time (such as "Soon" [page 248]) or location (such as "Close by" [page 249]). It can also be used to indicate fright or worry.

GRAMMAR AND SENTENCE STRUCTURE

ASL has its own grammar rules and sentence structure, which change depending on both the type of sentence and what you want to emphasize in it. Generally, in ASL you bring up the topic, then make a comment on it (similar to the structure of Spanish and Italian). The topic can be either the subject or the object of the sentence. For example, for the sentence "The dog caught the ball," "dog" is the subject, and "ball" is the object. Just like in English, whether you want to start your sentence with the subject or object is up to you—neither is right nor wrong. For instance, you could say "The dog caught the ball" or "The ball was caught by the dog," and both would be correct.

MOVIE

>> "The Movie is bad because it's boring" is signed as "Movie-Bad-Why?-Boring."

BAD

WHY?

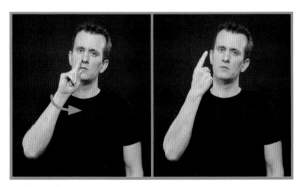

BORING

Subject-Verb-Object Structure

In proper ASL grammar, if start your sentence with the subject, you sign Subject-Verb-Object, similar to English: "Dog-Caught-Ball." If you are using adjectives, place them after what they're modifying, for example: "Dog-Brown-Caught-Ball-Blue." (Remember: It's like drawing. You have to draw the dog before you can make him brown!) Adverbs also go after their verb. Most ASL adverbs are the same sign as the adjective version—that is, "quick" and "quickly" are the same sign.

Object-Subject-Verb and Rhetorical Question Structure

But what if you'd like to place emphasis on the ball, not the dog? If starting a sentence with the object of a sentence (in this case, the ball), the proper ASL grammar is to sign Object-Subject-Verb: "Ball-Dog-Caught." This way of structuring a sentence is also useful if the subject (in this case, the dog) is doing more than one thing. For example, to sign "The dog ran after the ball and caught it," you'd simply add more verbs to the end, signing "Ball-Dog-Ran-Caught."

Rhetorical questions are often used in Object-Subject-Verb sentence structure after the verb to provide additional information. For example, to sign "The movie was bad because it was boring" using rhetorical question word order, you would sign, "Movie-Bad-Why?-Boring." If you wanted to sign, "He lost his keys because it was dark outside," you'd sign "Keys-Lost-Why?-Outside-Dark." When saying "Why?" make sure to use the same facial expression you would if you were speaking a rhetorical question: The eyebrows are raised as if you're making a point, not confused about something.

It might seem less straightforward, but rhetorical question word order comes in handy when you want to place emphasis on the information you're using to describe the object. In English, if someone said "How'd you like the movie?" you'd say, "I didn't like the movie because it was boring," not "I disliked the boring movie."

Asking Questions

Unlike in English, there's no need to change the structure of a sentence when asking a question. Whereas in English, you'd usually form a question as "Did the dog catch the ball?" rather than saying, "The dog caught the ball?" in ASL, you'd simply use the facial expression a person uses when asking a question, and sign "Dog-Caught-Ball" or "Ball-Dog-Caught" (depending on which sentence structure you're using).

Negation

To make a sentence negative in ASL, you can often just simply shake your head no while signing. For example, to sign "I don't work here" you would sign "I Work-Here" while shaking your head.

In ASL, we usually sign negation words at the end of sentences to emphasize negation. For instance, to sign "I never saw the movie," sign "Movie-See-Never." But it's also okay to sign the negation word before the subject ("Movie-Never-See").

Some phrases, like "don't like" and "don't want," have their own specific sign, as shown throughout the book.

Time

Unlike adjectives, time words are always placed either at the very beginning or very end of a sentence (again, depending on where you'd like to place emphasis). For example, to add "yesterday" to when you worked, sign "Yesterday-I Work" or "I Work-Yesterday."

"Being" Verbs

It's important to note that ASL has no "being" verbs: am, are, is, etc. So if you want to sign "I am a student," you'd simply sign "I-Student" and show with your facial expression that that's what you're saying, probably by nodding your head. To sign "He is happy," you'd just sign "He-Happy" with the proper facial expression.

TIPS FOR LEARNING ASL

Relax!

Try to loosen up, and don't overthink your signing! Although it's hard for new learners not to focus on making each sign properly, if you think too hard and focus on perfection, then you run the risk of looking stiff and robotic—and just as English speakers would rather listen to a good storyteller with a so-so grasp of English, someone who uses ASL would rather communicate with someone who uses facial expressions and eye contact even if they aren't the best at signing. So, try to sign smoothly even if you're signing slowly or using the alphabet to spell words you don't know. Signing with the right facial expressions will allow you to communicate much more effectively than signing perfectly, and will it give you more confidence!

It's important to try not to focus your attention on the hands of the person who is signing.

With ASL, it's essential to make eye contact, so that you can see the signer's facial expression and understand the context of what they're communicating. Not only is this context sometimes vital to the meaning of a sign, it can be a huge help to beginners—if you're making eye contact and interacting with someone, it's much easier to tell that they're telling a story about a cold winter rather than their new freezer (even though the signs are similar).

Be Social With the Deaf Community

The best way to improve your ASL is to be around the Deaf community! Not only will you get a chance to practice your ASL, you'll get more access to various ASL "accents," learn new Deaf idioms and slang (there are a few to get you started on pages 174–176), and improve your ability to understand what Deaf people are signing. You can find all sorts of different Deaf events around the US at the popular site DeafNation.com, which hosts Deaf Expos around the country several times a year with entertainment, workshops and exhibitions about Deaf culture. For more websites and ideas, see the Resources section at the end of the book.

Go Online

Online videos on sites like YouTube have been a huge asset to the Deaf community. On YouTube, you can find people using ASL for everything people use spoken English for: storytelling, reciting poetry, singing music, commenting on the news, or just blogging. Watching videos made by Deaf people is a great way to get better at your ASL comprehension and also see how different people have different styles of signing. You'll also find that different mediums even have different signing styles specific to their cultural expression. For instance, some Deaf artists like to sign using number- or alphabet-handshapes in certain ways to create unique stories and poems. See the Resources section for more information on how to find ASL videos on YouTube.

Learn About Deaf History and Culture

Spending time with the deaf community and going online are two great ways to learn about Deaf culture, which is essential to communicating effectively in ASL. The two go hand-in-hand, and the more you immerse yourself in Deaf history and culture, the easier it will be to understand some of the cultural differences between ASL and spoken English. For instance, some hearing people find Deaf culture to be more blunt in expressing things. However, when communicating in ASL, we usually bring up the point first, then explain the details. We feel we're simply not beating around the bush! This directness extends to a lot areas of Deaf culture—if we have to walk in between two people signing, for example, we probably won't wait for them to finish, then apologize and cut through. We'd just do it!

Understand ASL's Foundation

As I've explained, it's important to understand the parameters of ASL—properly using classifiers, handshapes, orientation, location, movement, and facial expressions—as well as grammar/sentence structure in order to improve your ASL skills and not look sloppy while you're doing it! Simply reading (and perhaps re-reading) this introduction will put you well on your way to becoming an effective ASL communicator and storyteller. Now it's time to learn some signs. Enjoy!

A

B

C

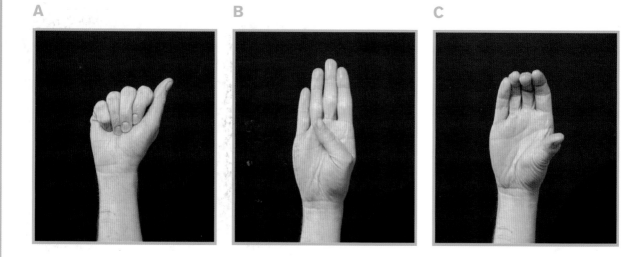

D

E

F

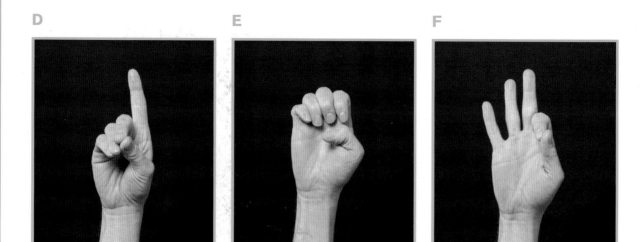

G

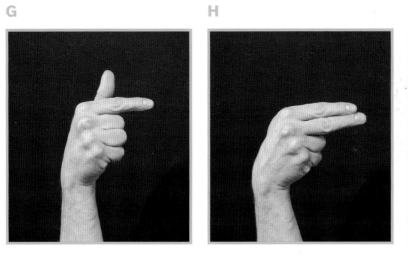

H

I

J

K

L

M

N

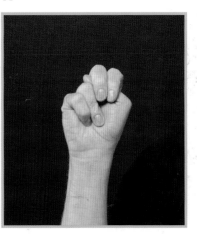

O

P

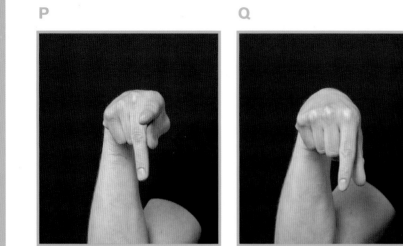

Q

R

S

T

U

V

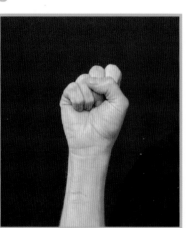

W

X

Y

Z

ZERO

ONE

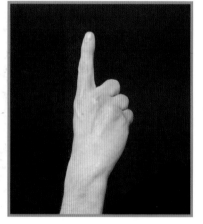

TWO

THREE

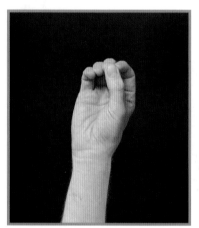

FOUR

FIVE

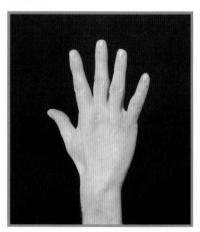

SIX

SEVEN

EIGHT

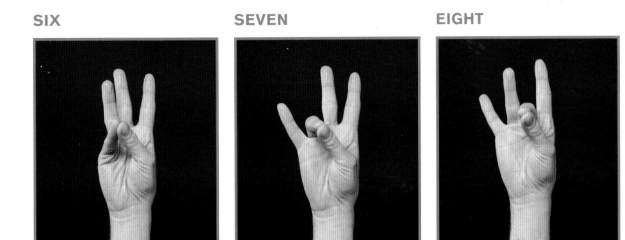

NINE

TEN

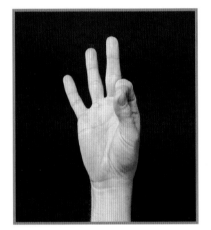

ELEVEN

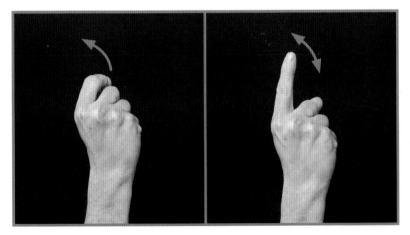

TWELVE

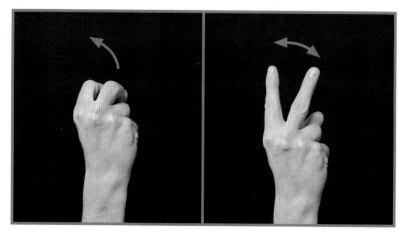

THIRTEEN

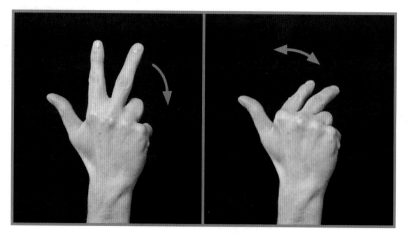

FOURTEEN

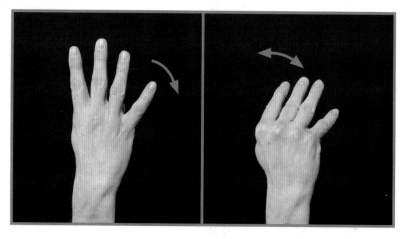

FIFTEEN

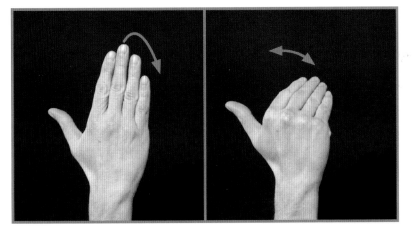

SIXTEEN

SEVENTEEN

EIGHTEEN

NINETEEN

TWENTY

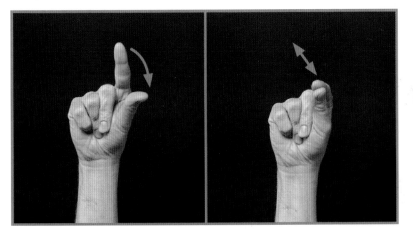

TWENTY-ONE

TWENTY-TWO

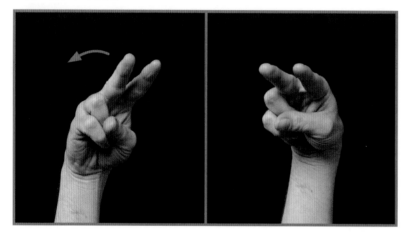

TWENTY-THREE

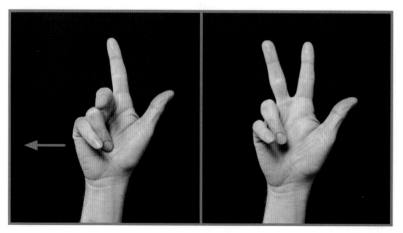

TWENTY-FOUR

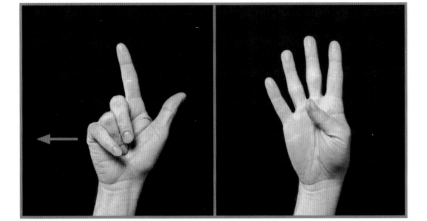

TWENTY-FIVE

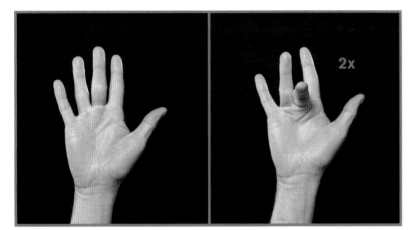

2x

TWENTY-SIX

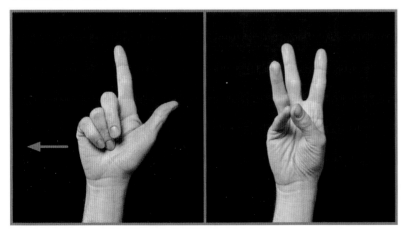

TWENTY-SEVEN

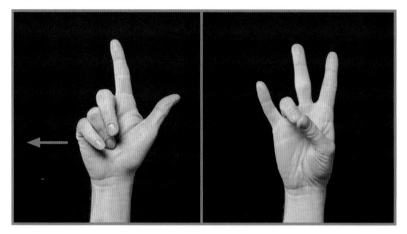

TWENTY-EIGHT

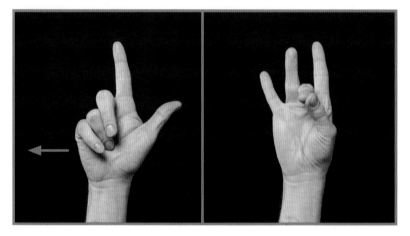

TWENTY-NINE

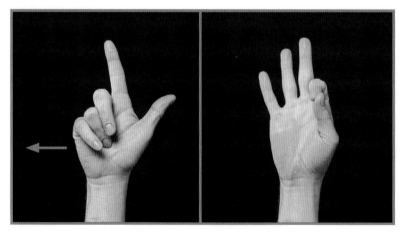

THIRTY

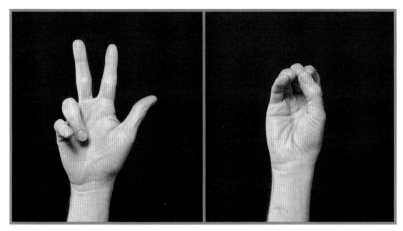

ONE HUNDRED

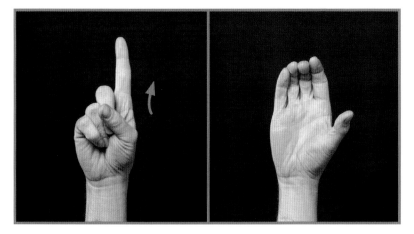

>> While moving your hand
back toward yourself,
change your handshape
from the numeral to a
loose "C."

FIVE HUNDRED

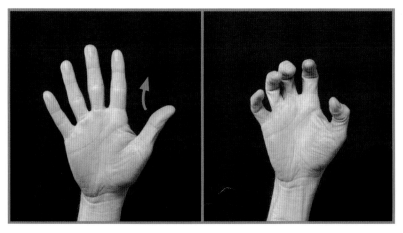

>> While moving your hand
back toward yourself,
change your handshape
from the numeral to a
loose "C."

ONE THOUSAND

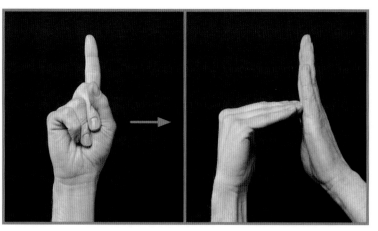

ONE MILLION

FIRST TIME

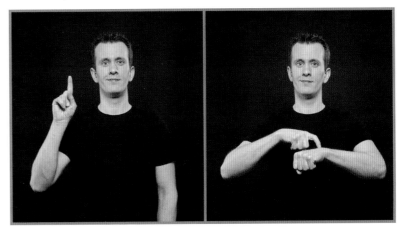

FIFTH TIME

SEVENTH TIME

general

IN

ON

AND

BUT

>> Make sure not to confuse this sign with "Different" (page 213), which is similar, but has a different facial expression.

KNOW

DON'T KNOW

>> Shake your head if desired. Make sure to emphasize your facial expression.

LIKE

>> Make sure to emphasize your facial expression.

DON'T LIKE

>> Sign "Like," then twist your hand downward and release your fingers.

GOOD

>> Make sure not to confuse this sign with "Thank you" (page 30) by signing only once and nodding.

BAD

>> Make sure to emphasize your facial expression.

essentials

YES

>> Nod if desired.

NO

>> Shake your head if desired. Make sure to emphasize your facial expression.

MAYBE

PLEASE

THANK YOU/YOU'RE WELCOME

>> Repeat.

THANK YOU SO MUCH!

>> Repeat as desired.

HELP YOU

>> Sign toward the person you're helping.

HELP ME

>> Sign away from the person who is helping you.

EXCUSE ME

SORRY

>> Repeat if desired.
Make sure to emphasize
your facial expression.

WANT

>> Close your fingers while
moving your hands inward.

DON'T WANT

>> Make sure to emphasize
your facial expression.

NEED

>> Move just your hand and emphasize your facial expression. Increase the sign speed to indicate "Really need."

BATHROOM

AGAIN

>> Repeat to sign "Repeatedly."

MY NAME IS...

>> Sign "My," then "Name"

NICE TO MEET YOU

>> Sign "Nice," then sign "Meet." When signing "Meet," move your dominant hand toward the person your're meeting.

pronouns

HE/SHE/IT

>> Sign toward the person you're referring to, if possible.

THEY

>> Sign toward the person you're referring to, if possible.

US/WE

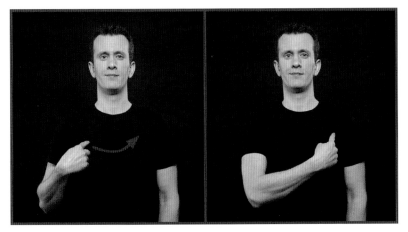

>> Modify this sign by signing in a larger arc to indicate a larger group of people.

HIS/HERS/ITS

>> Sign toward the person you're referring to, if possible.

YOUR

>> Sign toward the person you're referring to, if possible.

OUR

MY

MYSELF

questions

WHO

>> Repeatedly flick your index finger. Make sure to emphasize your facial expression.

WHAT

>> Make sure to emphasize your facial expression.

WHEN

>> Circle the index finger of your dominant hand around your non-dominant hand, ending with your fingers touching. Make sure to emphasize your facial expression.

WHERE

>> Make sure to emphasize your facial expression.

WHY

>> Make sure to emphasize your facial expression.

WHICH

>> Repeat. Make sure to emphasize your facial expression.

HOW

>> Make sure to emphasize your facial expression.

communication

DEAF

>> Moving your index finger in the opposite direction, from chin to ear, is also an acceptable way to sign "Deaf."

HEARING

>> Move your index finger in a circle near your mouth.

TEXT (Verb)

>> Sign toward the person you're texting if possible.

TEXT (Noun)

>> Move your thumbs like you're texting while alternating moving your hands up and down.

EMAIL (Noun)

EMAIL (Verb)

>> Sign toward the person you're emailing if possible.

general

YESTERDAY

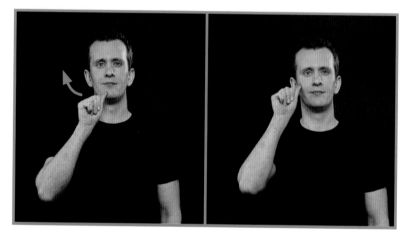

TODAY

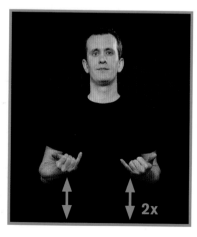

>> Make sure not to confuse this sign with "Now" (page 248) by repeating this sign once.

TOMORROW

TONIGHT

DAY

WEEK

MONTH

YEAR

>> Move your dominant hand up and around your other hand. Repeat to sign "Years and years."

LAST WEEK

>> Move your dominant hand in an arc away from your palm.

NEXT WEEK

>> Make sure to move your hand in an arc.

LAST MONTH

NEXT MONTH

LAST YEAR

>> Flick your index finger up
and down while you sign.

NEXT YEAR

days of the week

MONDAY

TUESDAY

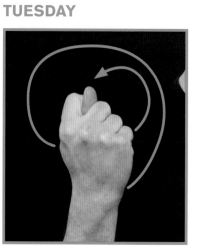

WEDNESDAY

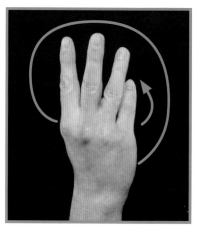

THURSDAY

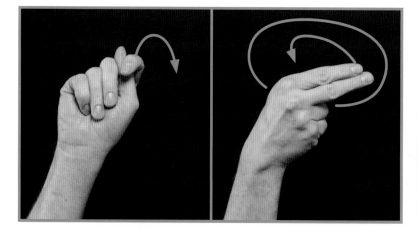

FRIDAY

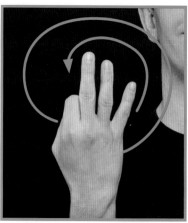

SATURDAY

SUNDAY

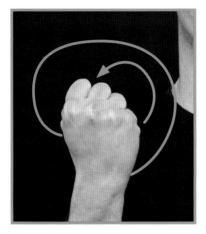

>> Move your hands in an arc, toward your chest and down, then forward again.

times

ALL NIGHT

>> Move your dominant hand around the outside of your other hand. Make sure to emphasize your facial expression.

ALL DAY

>> Make sure to emphasize your facial expression.

EVERY DAY

>> Make sure to emphasize your facial expression.

Possible Classifier Examples >> **EVERY DAY**

Every Monday

Every Saturday

Every Wednesday and Friday

EVERY WEEK

>> Make sure to emphasize your facial expression. This sign differs from "Week" (page 43) in that it's repeated.

EVERY MONTH

>> Repeatedly make the sign for "Month" by moving your dominant index finger up and down your other index finger continuously in a circle. Make sure to emphasize your facial expression.

EVERY YEAR

>> Flick your index finger while you sign, and emphasize your facial expression.

FIVE O'CLOCK

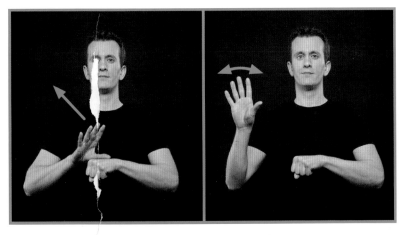

ELEVEN O'CLOCK

>> Make the sign for "Eleven" (page 17) after moving your dominant arm.

MIDNIGHT

>> Flick the sign for "Twelve" (page 18) a few times.

NOON

>> Move arm back to front and repeat.

FAMILY & FRIENDS

family

MOTHER

FATHER

WIFE

HUSBAND

CHILD

CHILDREN

BABY

SON

>> Move your dominant hand as if saluting from your forehead to your non-dominant hand.

DAUGHTER

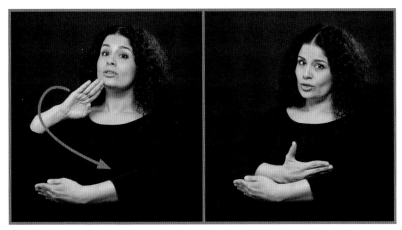

>> Move your dominant hand as if saluting from your forehead to the crook of your other arm.

SISTER

BROTHER

>> Change your handshape from "A" to "1" as you move your arm.

GRANDMOTHER

GRANDFATHER

AUNT

UNCLE

NIECE

NEPHEW

COUSIN (Girl)

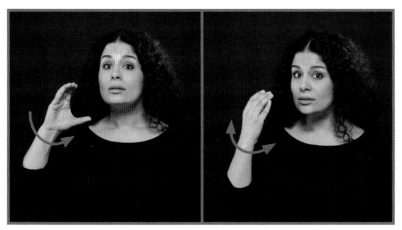

COUSIN (Boy)

>>The sign for a female cousin (above) is made by forming a "C" near your chin. A boy cousin is made by forming a "C" near your forehead. To sign "Cousins" in general (boy and girl), sign near the middle of your face.

friends

FRIEND

>>Grip hooked index finger with the other, then switch your hands' palm orientations repeatedly.

GIRLFRIEND

>>Sign "Girl," then "Friend."

BOYFRIEND

>>Sign "Boy," then "Friend."

GOOD FRIEND

BEST FRIEND

GREW UP

ROOMMATE

2x

relationships

RELATIONSHIP

MARRIED

DIVORCED

SEPARATED

body parts

ARM / OTHER BODY PARTS

>> This shows "Arm."
For other body parts,
simply point to them.

HEAD

MOUTH

>> Draw a circle
around your mouth.

TEETH

NOSE

HEART

LUNGS

2x

medical

HEALTH

AMBULANCE

>> Twist your hands in the air.

DOCTOR

NURSE

HOSPITAL

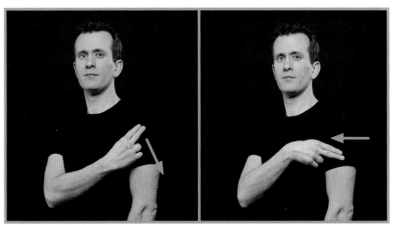

PHYSICAL

>> Same sign as "Body" and "Human."

THERAPY

>> Same sign as "Help," but
with the "T" handshape,
and repeated.

ALLERGY

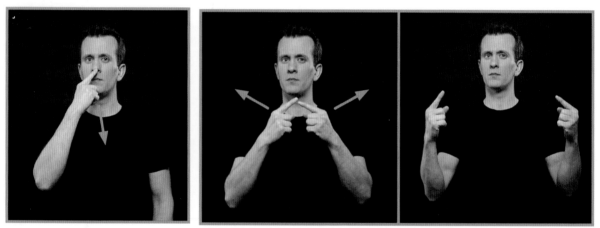

PERIOD

>> Make an "A" handshape.

PREGNANT

MEDICINE

SHOT

PILL

TAKE THE PILL

>> Make sure to sign only once.

BORN

LIVE

DIE

symptoms & ailments

SICK/DISEASE

HEADACHE

2x

PAIN/HURT

>> Make sure to emphasize your facial expression to show how much it hurts! Modify this sign by indicating it near different body parts, as shown below.

TOOTHACHE

STOMACHACHE

COLD (Sickness)

>> Squeeze an "X" handshape and your thumb while moving downward. Repeat.

COUGH

>> Hit your chest twice in
a circular movement,
as if you're coughing.

SNEEZE

>> Make the facial
expression you would
make when sneezing
and nod your head.

FEVER

BLEEDING

BLOOD

>> Wiggle your fingers while moving them downward.

SPRAIN

BREAK

general

HOUSE

>> Modify this sign by using a facial expression to show the size of the house.

HOME

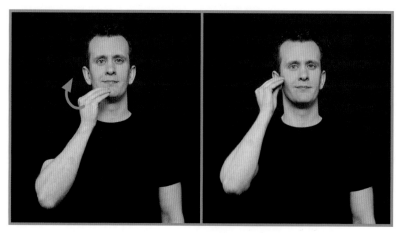

RUNNING OUT OF...

>> Make sure to emphasize your facial expression.

SMARTPHONE

TABLET COMPUTER

2x

parts of your home

ROOM

>> Modify this sign by signing it in the shape of the room and/or emphasizing your facial expression according to the size of the room.

DOOR

2x

>> Instead of repeating, you can modify this sign by signing only once, to indicate either the door opening or the door closing (depending on your movement).

FLOOR

WINDOW

2x

Possible Classifier Examples >> WINDOW

Open Window

Possible Classifier Examples >> WINDOW

Close Window

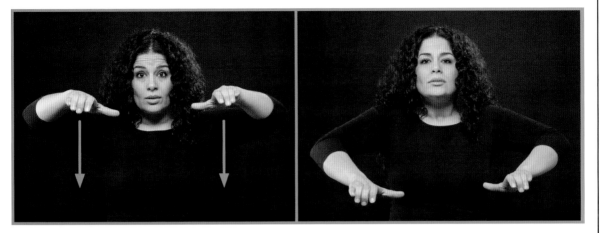

Open Curtains

Close Curtains

WALL

>> This also can be
used as a classifier.

Possible Classifier Examples >> WALL

Long Wall

>> Make sure to use
a "Puff" non-manual
sign (as shown).

∨
∨ Start by signing "Wall,"
then turn one hand outward
while not dropping either
hand. Modify this sign by
signing the shape or size of
the wall.

Corner of the Wall

GO UPSTAIRS

>> Flick two fingers while moving your hand upward.

GO DOWNSTAIRS

>> Flick two fingers while moving your hand downward.

furniture

FURNITURE

REFRIGERATOR

>> Make sure not to confuse this sign with "Cold" (page 185) or "Winter" (page 183) by keeping your hands closer together and shaking them twice. This sign can also be signed with the "1" handshape on both hand.

CHAIR

2x

>> Repeat to sign "Chair."
Sign once for "Sit."

Possible Classifier Example >> CHAIR

Group of Chairs

>> Make the sign for "Chair" (above) in the location of the chairs. For instance, for four chairs in a circle, make the sign for chair four times, while moving hands in a circular shape.

TABLE

>> Bring your dominant arm down and repeat.

Possible Classifier Examples >> TABLE

Circular Table

Rectangular Table

>> Move hands in a different shape for a differently shaped table.

COUCH

Possible Classifier Example >> COUCH

L-Shaped Couch

BED

DRAWER

>> Move your hands toward your body and back again. This is the same sign as "Dresser."

Possible Classifier Examples >> DRAWER

Close Drawer

Open Drawer

>> Move open hands away from your body as if closing a drawer.

>> Move cupped hands toward your body as if opening a drawer.

CABINET

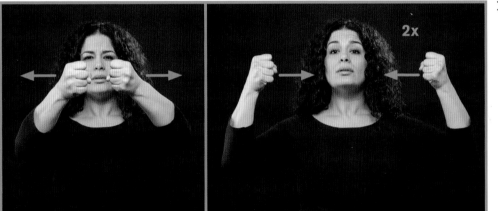

>>Turn hands outward, then inward again and repeat.

Possbile Classifier Example >> CABINET

Open and Close Cabinet

clothes

CLOSET

>> Make an "X" handshape over a "1" handshape, like a hanger. Then repeat and move outward.

Possible Classifier Example >> CLOSET

Hanging up Clothes in the Closet

>> Make a "Y" handshape and move right or left to indicate the length of the closet. Modify your facial expression to show the quality of the clothes.

CLOTHES

>> Make sure not to confuse this sign with "Dress" by repeating it.

LAUNDRY

SHIRT

DRESS

PANTS

SKIRT

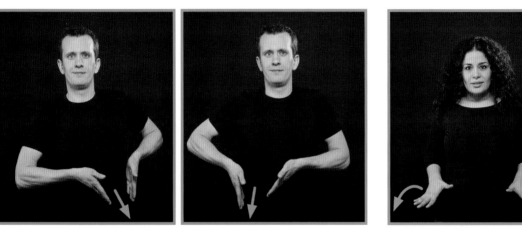

SUIT

HOODIE/SWEATSHIRT

TANK TOP

>> Make a "G" handscape with both hands, like the straight lines of straps. Repeat.

UNDERWEAR

BRA

SOCKS

shoes & accessories

SHOES

FLIP-FLOPS/SANDALS

HIGH HEELS

SCARF

>> Move your dominant hand as if you're wrapping a scarf around your other arm.

COAT

>> Make an "A" handshape while moving your hands like you're putting on a coat.

GLOVES

>> Repeat on other hand. Sign in the opposite direction (up your hand rather than down) to indicate taking gloves off.

WINTER HAT

BASEBALL CAP

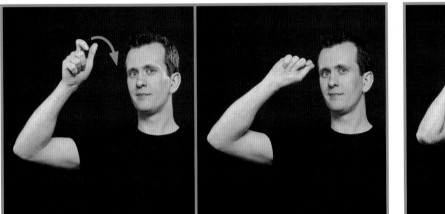

HEADPHONES

RING

EARRING

>> Open and close your index finger and thumb like you're clipping an earring on. Sign only once to sign "Putting an earring on."

NECKLACE

>> Signing this in the opposite direction is also acceptable.

BRACELET

>> Repeat to sign "Bracelet." Sign once to sign "Putting a bracelet on."

pets

PET

CAT

DOG

>> Snap you middle finger and thumb twice.

BIRD

>> Flick index and thumb to indicate the beak and repeat.

TURTLE

>> Put your non-dominant hand over your dominant hand like a turtle's shell, and wiggle your dominant thumb like a turtle's head.

RABBIT

MOUSE

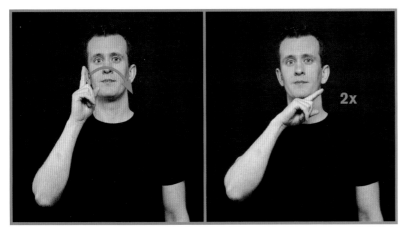

SNAKE

>> This sign is only for the noun only. Modify this sign by changing your handshape to show the shape or length of the snake.

general

APPOINTMENT

WALK

Possible Classifier Examples >> WALKING

One Person Walking

>> Make sure to emphasize your facial expression. Modify this sign by signing in the direction of walking.

Two People Walking

>> Make sure to emphasize your facial expression. Modify this sign by signing in the direction of walking.

One Person Walking Variation

>> Make sure to emphasize your facial expression. Modify this sign by signing in the direction of walking.

directions

STOP

>> Make sure to emphasize your facial expression.

GO

>> Modify this sign by signing in the direction of movement.

LEFT

RIGHT

NORTH

SOUTH

EAST

WEST

ADDRESS

>> Make sure not to confuse this sign with "Live" (page 64) by moving your hands in an outward arc to your shoulders.

shopping

SHOPPING

Possible Classifier Examples >> SHOPPING

Shopping a Lot

>> Increase your speed as you sign and use a "Puff," "Cha," or "Soa" facial expression (page 8).

Shopping a Little

>> Make sure to decrease your speed as you sign and make an "Mmm" facial expression (as shown).

HOW MUCH

>> Modify this sign by using a facial expression to show how much (page 8.)

COST/PRICE

>> Make an "X" handshape while signing.

CREDIT CARD

CASH/MONEY

DOLLARS

CENTS

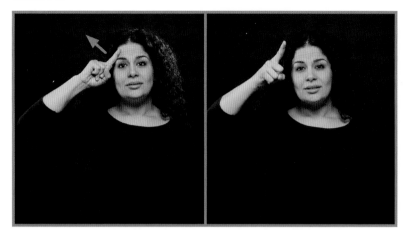

$1

$6

>> Twist your wrist twice.

$9

>> Twist your wrist twice.
Show other dollar values
by making the handshape
of the number and twisting
your wrist twice.

WALLET

BAG

>> Same sign as "Purse."

STORE

>> Twist your wrists twice.

transportation

CAR

TRUCK

>> Make sure not to confuse this sign with "Car" by placing your hands farther apart.

DRIVING

>> Modify this sign by signing toward the direction of driving. To sign "Driving," repeat.

Possible Classifier Examples >> DRIVING

Driving on Bumpy Road

>> Make sure to make the "Puff" facial expression, as shown. Modify this sign by signing in the direction of driving.

Driving on Hilly Road

>> Make sure to make the appropriate facial expression dpending on how hilly the road is (page 8). Modify this sign by signing toward the direction of driving.

Parking

>> Modify this sign by signing in the direction of parking.

Possible Classifier Examples >> DRIVING

Row of Cars Parking

>> Make a "Puff"
   or "Cha" facial
   expression
   (page 8) or blow
   a raspberry as
   you sign.

TRAIN

2x

SUBWAY

>> Make a "Y" handshape
   as you sign.

2x

Possible Classifier Example >> SUBWAY
Subway Going Underground

>> Make sure to make a "Puff" facial expression (as shown) as you sign.

AIRPLANE

2x

Possible Classifier Examples >> AIRPLANE
Airplane Landing

>> Modify this sign by moving hands in the direction the airplane is landing.

Possible Classifier Examples >> AIRPLANE

Airplane Departing

>> Modify this sign by moving hands in the direction the airplane is departing.

FLY

>> Modify this sign by moving hands in the direction the airplane is flying.

TICKETS

>> Sign twice for noun. Sign once for the verb "Ticketed."

places

PLACE

VACATION

BEACH

>> Move your dominant hand like waves crashing on a beach.

RESTAURANT

>> Make an "R" handshape while moving your hand down each side of your face.

BAR

COURT

>> This sign also means "Judge" in some regions.

CHURCH

TEMPLE

MOSQUE

STATE

>> Place an "S" handshape against your upper palm, then move the "S" out and down to the lower part of your palm.

COUNTRY

>> Move your dominant hand in a circular motion in front of your elbow twice.

USA/AMERICA

>> Interlock your fingers and move your hands in a circular motion twice.

general

SCHOOL

COLLEGE

MEETING

WORK

Possbile Classifier Example >> WORK

Working a Lot

>> Make sure to emphasize your facial expression, and repeat the sign as desired to indicate more work.

SCHEDULE

>> Move your dominant hand down and then across your other palm.

PROJECT

>> Making a "P" handshape, bring your dominant hand up and over the other hand's palm, then use just your pinky to bring it back down the other side. (Note: Body movement is just to show back of hands and not part of sign.)

COPY

>> Modify this sign by signing away from what you are copying.

INTERNET

>> Twist your non-dominant wrist twice. To sign "Website," repeat the handshape "W" three times.

equipment & supplies

COMPUTER

MACHINE

COPY MACHINE

>> Repeat more than once
   to sign "Scanning."

PAPER

Possible Classifier Example >> **PAPER**

Stack of Papers

>> Make sure to make a "Puff" or "Cha" facial expression (page 8).

PEN

>> This sign can also be used for "Write."

BOOK

Possible Classifier Example >> BOOK

Books on Shelves

>> Modify this sign by signing toward the shelf to indicate its location and/or by changing your facial expression to indicate amount of books.

majors & subjects

MATH

SCIENCE

>> Move hands in alternating circles with your thumbs going toward your chest and repeat.

HISTORY   ## ECONOMICS

ART

>> Same sign as the noun "Drawing." To sign the verb "Drawing," repeat.

SOCIAL STUDIES

GYM

LAW

the classroom

TEACHER

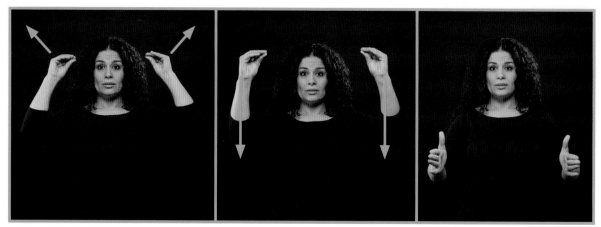

STUDENT

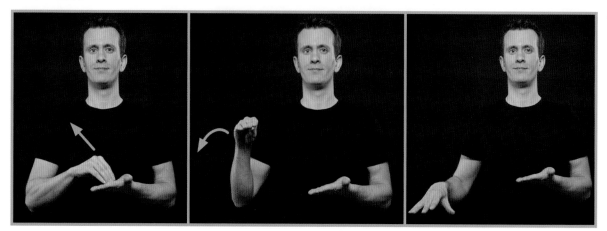

LEARN

LEARNING

>> Make the sign for "Learn" and repeat.

CLASS

PASS

FAIL

>> Make a "K" handshape and slide across your palm.

QUESTION

>> Repeat as desired.

2x

ANSWER

>> Modify this sign by signing toward the person who is answering or being answered.

RIGHT/CORRECT

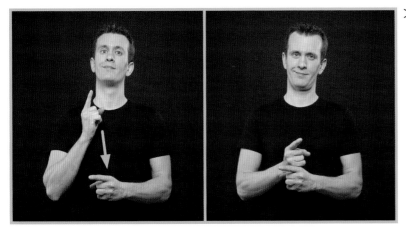

>> Make a "C" handshape with both hands and touch.

WRONG

HOMEWORK

TEST

>> Change your handshape from "1" to "X" as you move your hands down.

STUDY

>> Wiggle your fingers as you move your hand downward.

READ

business

BUSINESS

>> To sign "Busy,"
repeat several times,
making sure to
add an appropriate
facial expression.

OFFICE

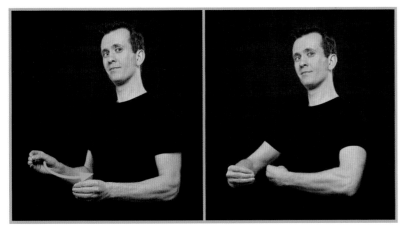

ACCOUNTING

>> Same sign as "Count."

MARKETING

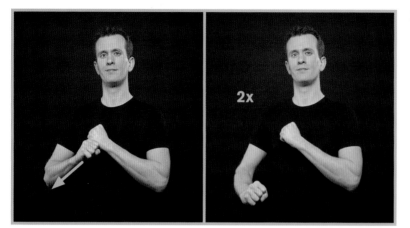

>> Repeat at least once.

SELL

>> Bend your hands down and pivot them away from your body. Sign once for "Sell" and twice for "Store."

BOSS

>> Same sign as "Coach."

COWORKER

>> First sign "Co-" by meshing your hands together, then "Work" (page 105), then "-er," which is made by facing your palms toward each other and moving your hands down.

CLIENT/CUSTOMER

PRESENTATION

>> To sign "Presenting," repeat at least twice.

jobs

HIRED

>> Modify this sign by signing toward the person who's been hired.

FIRED

>> Modify this sign by signing toward the person who's been fired.

LAYOFF

>> Modify this sign by signing toward the person who's been laid off.

PRESIDENT

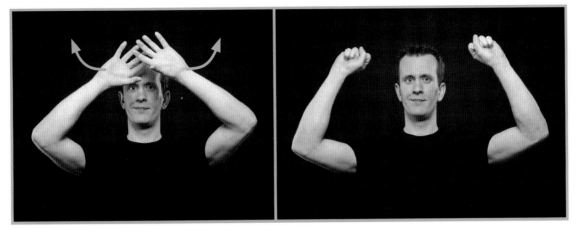

VICE PRESIDENT

>> Make the handshape for "V," then "P."

LAWYER

SECRETARY

>> Make an "H" handshape as you sign. In ASL, it's still customary to use "secretary" rather than "assistant."

PHOTOGRAPHER

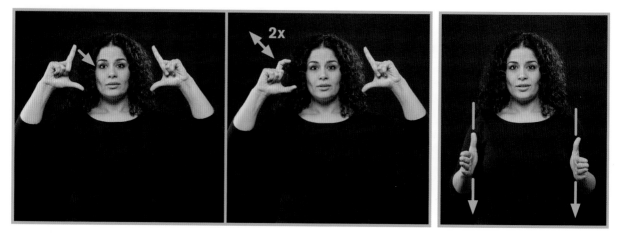

general

FOOD

EAT

ORDER (FOOD)

>> Modify this sign by signing toward the person you're ordering from.

HUNGRY

STARVING

>> Make sure to emphasize how hungry you are with your facial expression!

THIRSTY

>> Make sure to emphasize your facial expression. Repeat continuously to indicate extreme thirst.

VEGETARIAN

>> Sign "Vegetables" (page 136), then move hands downward with palms facing inward to indicate a person who does something.

meals

BREAKFAST

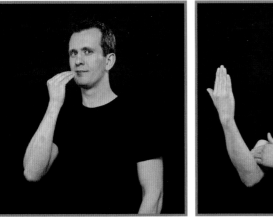

>> Sign "Eat,"
then "Morning."

LUNCH

>> Sign "Eat,"
then "Noon."

DINNER

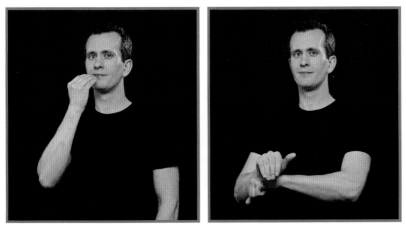

>> Sign "Eat,"
then "Night."

SNACK

SANDWICH

PIZZA

EGG

CEREAL

>> Move hand in a scooping motion while making a "C" handshape.

PANCAKES

>> Move your hand as if you're flipping a pancake.

TOAST

>> Twist your non-dominant hand into a "B" handshape after the other hand touches it.

PASTA

>> With your pinkies extended, bring your hands in, then move in a circle.

TACO

>> Make sure not to confuse this sign with "Hot dog" (page 131) by using the proper handshape.

SALAD

meat, grains, & dairy

MEAT

>> Lightly shake
your hands.

CHICKEN

TURKEY

FISH

HAMBURGER

>> Cup your palms together as if making a patty, then reverse and cup them with the other hand on top.

PORK

SAUSAGE

>> Open and close your fists as if squeezing out sausage links while moving your hands in opposite directions.

HOT DOG

>> Use a "1" handshape for the hot dog and a cupped "C" handshape for the bun. Make sure not to confuse with "Taco" (page 128).

BACON

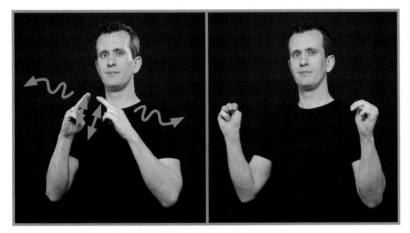

>> Flick two fingers on each hand while moving them in opposite directions.

BREAD

RICE

>> Flutter the fingers of
your top hand.

BEANS

CHEESE

>> Keep your palms together
while your fingers swing
back and forth twice.

produce

FRUIT

>> Use an "F" handshape while moving your hand along the edge of your cheek and repeat.

APPLE

>> Use an "X" handshape pressed against your cheek while twisting your wrist. Repeat.

ORANGE

LEMON/LIME

>> Make an "L" handshape with your thumb on your chin, then wiggle your index finger.

GRAPES

>> Touch the back of your non-dominant hand with your dominant fingers several times as you move them down the hand.

CHERRIES

>> Twist your wrist while holding each finger.

STRAWBERRY

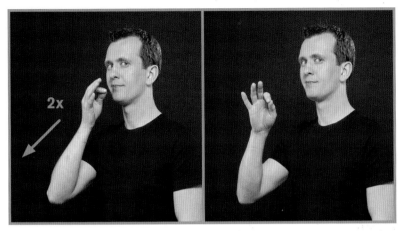

>> Twist your hand while moving downward. Repeat.

BANANA

>> Move your hand down like you're peeling a banana.

MELON

>> Flick your non-dominant hand with your dominant middle finger and thumb twice.

TOMATO

>> On your non-dominant hand, touch your thumb to your fingers. With your dominant hand, touch your index finger to your chin, then move it down, touching your non-dominant hand on the way.

VEGETABLES

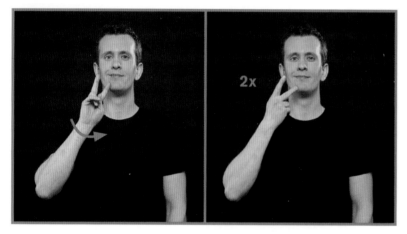

>> Touch a "V" handshape to the side of your face, then flip your hand so the "V" is facing the other direction.

CARROT

>> Move your hand to your mouth like you're eating a carrot.

POTATO

ONION

>> Make an "X" handshape against the edge of your eye and twist your arm twice.

CORN

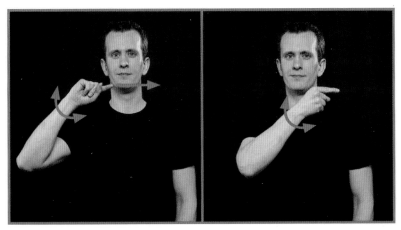

>> Make sure to keep twisting your hand while moving from right to left (or vice versa).

desserts

DESSERT

>> While holding up your pinky and thumb, touch your other fingers together and repeat.

COOKIE

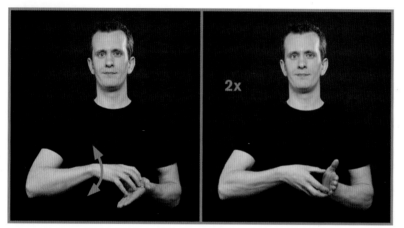

>> Bring your dominant hand down to your other hand and twist like you're cutting out cookie dough and repeat.

ICE CREAM

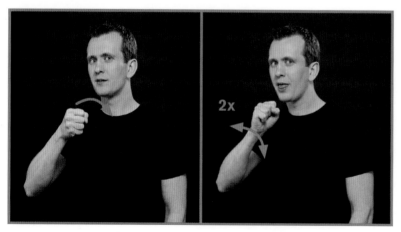

>> Bring your fist up to your mouth and twist your wrist, then repeat the sign like you're eating ice cream!

PIE

>> Move your hand like you're slicing a pie.

CANDY

>> Twist your wrist twice.

CHOCOLATE

>> Twist your dominant hand while making a "C" handshape on top of your other hand and repeat.

drinks

DRINK

>> Repeat when signing "Drink." Sign only once for "Drinking."

WATER

>> Tap a "W" handshape on your chin twice.

COFFEE

>> Twist your hand while making an "S" handshape on top of your other hand and repeat.

TEA

"ICED"

MILK

>> Make a "C" handshape,
then close it into an "S"
handshape twice.

JUICE

>> Make a "J" shape/movement by your mouth.

WINE

>> Make a "W" handshape and move in a circle near your face. Repeat.

SODA/POP

>> Making a "hole" with your non-dominant hand, dip the middle finger of your dominant hand into it, bring up, then place your palm on it.

BEER

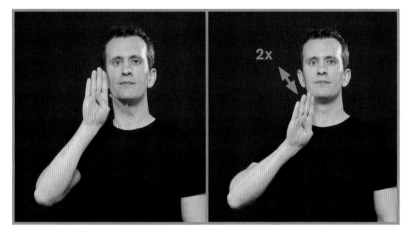

COCKTAIL/ALCOHOL

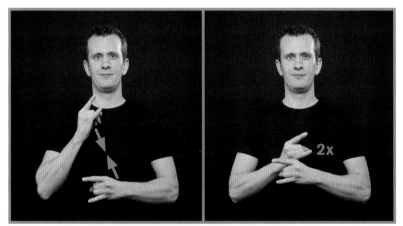

SHOT

cooking

COOK

BAKE

KITCHEN

SAUCE

>> Move your dominant hand in a circle from back to front over your palm while making a "Y" or "A" handshape.

SALT

>> Make "V" handshapes with both hands, then tap the fingers of your dominant hand on top of the fingers of your non-dominant hand. Repeat.

PEPPER

SPICY

>> Flutter your fingers as you sign and alter your facial expression depending on how spicy the food is.

SWEET

>> Sign once for "Sweet." Repeat for "Sugar."

SOUR/BITTER

>> Alter your facial expression depending on how bitter the food is.

tableware

DISH

>> Modify this sign by making your hands in the shape of the plate.

BOWL

>> Move both hands upward like the shape of a bowl.

CUP

FORK

KNIFE

SPOON

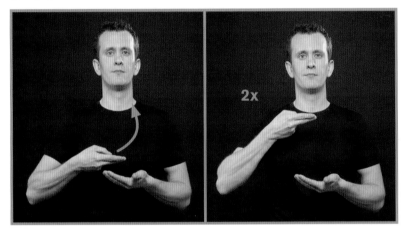

>> Repeat to sign "Spoon."
   Sign only once for "Soup."

NAPKIN

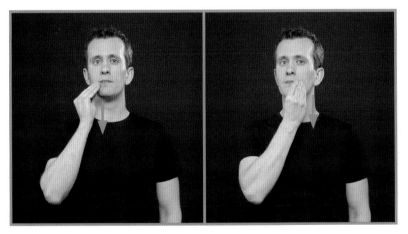

>> ACTIVITIES

online

UPLOAD

DOWNLOAD/STREAMING

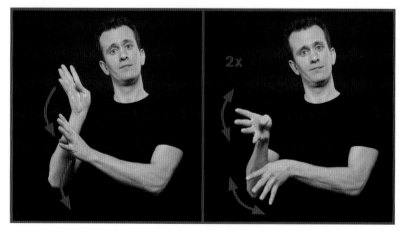

WIFI

FACEBOOK

INSTAGRAM

TWITTER

>> Similar to "Bird"
(page 86).

HASHTAG

leisure

WATCHING

>> Such as a TV show or movie. Repeat to sign "Watching." Sign only once for "Watch.

MOVIE

TV

GAME

PLAYING

>> Such as children playing.

SHOW

>> Same sign as "Play" or "Theater."

ACTOR

>> Sign "Show" twice then move hands down to indicate someone who does something.

DIRECTOR

AUDIENCE

>> Change your facial expression (page 8) to indicate the size of the audience.

DANCE

>> Repeat to sign "Dance." Continue repeating for "Dancing."

MUSIC

>> Repeat to sign "Music" or "Concert." Continue repeating to sign "Music is playing" and add an appropriate facial expression to describe the music.

SING

>> Wiggle fingers and repeat. Continue repeating to sign "Singing."

RADIO

>> Note that this sign should be repeated only once; when continuously repeated and made with the wrong facial expression it means "Crazy"!

sports

SPORT

MATCH

>> Move your hands toward each other while making a competitive-looking facial expression.

1ST (place)

2ND (place)

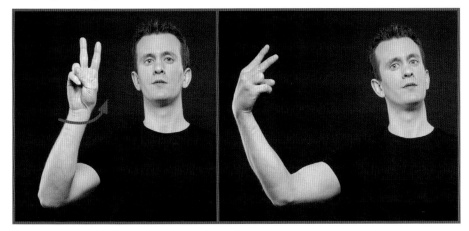

3RD (place)

BASKETBALL

BASEBALL

SOCCER

FOOTBALL

HOCKEY

>> Use an "X" handshape.

VOLLEYBALL

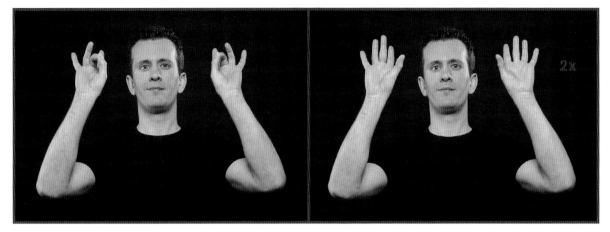

WRESTLING

SKIING

>> Make sure to move both hands simultaneously.

SNOWBOARDING

>> Make sure to move both hands simultaneously.

ICE-SKATE

>> Make sure NOT to move both hands simultaneously.

ROLLER-SKATING

>> Make sure NOT to move both hands simultaneously.

BIKING

>> Repeat and sign in a smaller space for "Bike." Repeat continuously in a larger space for "Biking."

RUNNING

>> Continuously flick your index finger while your hands are moving.

Possible Classifier Example >> RUNNING

Running Heavily

>> Make a "1" handshape, and increase your speed if desired. Make sure to emphasize your facial expression.

GYM

SWIMMING

WORKOUT

>> Move your hands like you're bench-pressing. Repeat.

Possible Classifier Example >> **FISHING**

FISHING

Caught a Big Fish

>> Sign toward the location you caught the fish. Make a "Puff" facial expression (as shown) to show you're catching a big one!

holidays

HOLIDAY

>> Make sure NOT to move both hands simultaneously.

NEW YEAR'S

>> Sign "New," then "Year."

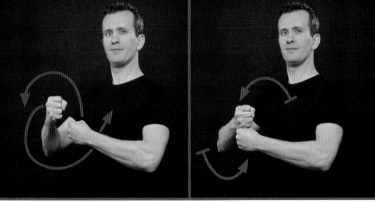

VALENTINE'S DAY

>> Sign "Heart" as shown, then "Day" (page 43).

EASTER

>> Twist your hands twice.

PASSOVER

RAMADAN

4TH OF JULY

>> Twist your hand once, then finger-spell "July."

FIREWORKS

>> Make a "1" handshape, then, while moving it upward, change it as if your hand is exploding.

ROSH HASHANAH

YOM KIPPUR

HALLOWEEN

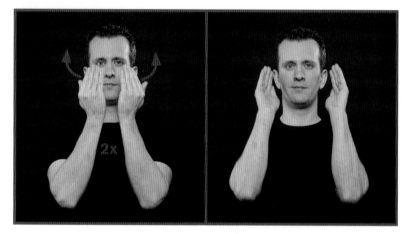

>> Make your hands like a mask.

THANKSGIVING

HANUKKAH

CHRISTMAS

>> Twist your hand while moving your arm in an arc.

SANTA CLAUS

>> Make your hands like the shape of a beard.

ELF

>> Make your hands like the shapes of elf ears.

BIRTHDAY

ANNIVERSARY

BAR/BAT MITZVAH

GIFT

>> Sign toward the person you're giving the gift to.

general

YOU'RE INVITED

>> Sign toward the person you're inviting.

FUN

>> Touch the middle and index fingers of your dominant hand to your nose, then bring them down to the index and middle fingers of your non-dominant hand.

HANG OUT

>> Move both hands in alternating circles toward and away from the body. Make sure NOT to move both hands simultaneously.

CHAT

2x

>> Repeat continuously to sign "Chatting."

PICTURE

PHOTO/CAMERA

>> Flick your dominant index finger like you're pressing the shutter on a camera. Sign toward the direction you're taking the picture.

Possible Classifier Example >> PHOTO

Selfie

small talk

COOL!

>> Wiggle your fingers and modify your facial expression depending on how cool it is.

WHAT'S UP?

AWESOME

>> Move your hands in an arc, inward and down. You can also sign this by moving your hands in the opposite direction (outward and up).

AMAZING!

>> Emphasize your facial expression by looking like your eyes are popping!

AMAZING/SURPRISE

>> Make sure to emphasize your facial expression.

LOVE IT!

>> Make sure to emphasize your facial expression. Look in the direction of what you love.

DANG/DARN/DAMN

>> Make sure to emphasize your facial expression.

deaf slang

CHAMP!

>> Used to express how great/ amazing something is, e.g., "The food is so good, CHAMP!" or "This show is CHAMP!"

DO-DO (Whatcha Doing?)

>> Make sure to emphasize that you're asking a question by squeezing your eyebrows together. This sign means "What are you up to?" but can also mean a diversion to pass the time, e.g., "I'll just keep myself busy by do-do."

FINISH (Enough!)

>> This sign is similar to the traditional sign for "Finish" except it uses one hand and is commonly used in conversation. Make sure to emphasize your angry facial expression.

PAH

>> Used to express "Finally," e.g., "I worked all night, but Pah! Finished!"

TRUE BIZ (For Real?)

>> This sign means "for real?" but can also be used as "actually" or "literally" depending on your facial expression.

POW-POW

>> Used to express doing something easily, e.g., "It only took me 5 minutes to finish my work, POW-POW!"

TRAIN GO SORRY (Missed the Boat)

>> Deaf expression that means the same thing as as "you missed the boat," e.g., if you entered into a conversation late and asked what you missed, someone might tell you, "train go sorry."

dating

SINGLE

DATE

GAY

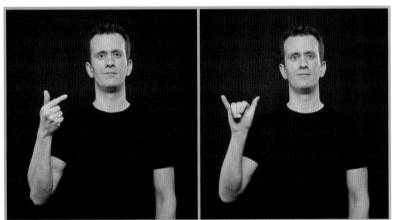

STRAIGHT

BISEXUAL

>> Sign "B," then "I."

SWEETHEART

LOVE

FALL IN LOVE

>> Make sure to emphasize your facial expression. Modify this sign by signing toward the person or thing you fell in love with.

FLIRT

>> Wiggle your fingers.

KISS

>> Sign once for "Kiss." Repeat to sign "Kissing."

SEX

>> Make an "X" handshape while signing downward in a small arc from the top of your cheek to your chin.

HOOK UP

general

INDOOR

>> Make sure not to confuse this sign with "In" by repeating it.

OUTDOOR

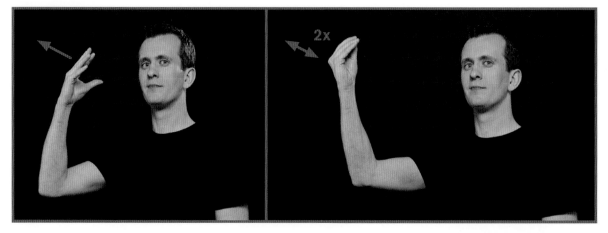

NATURE

>> Make a circle with your index and middle fingers before bringing them to your non-dominant hand.

MOON

STAR

seasons

SEASON

SPRING

>> Same sign as the noun "Plant. "Make sure not to confuse this sign with "Grow" by repeating it.

SUMMER

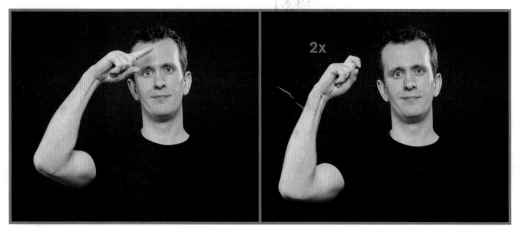

FALL

2x

WINTER

2x

>> Make sure not to confuse this sign with "Cold" by repeating it.

weather

WEATHER

WARM

>> Make sure to emphasize your facial expression.

HOT

>> Make sure to emphasize your facial expression.

COOL

>> Move your hand like you're using a fan. Make sure to emphasize your facial expression.

COLD

>> Make sure not to confuse this sign with "Winter" and "Refrigerator" by emphasizing your facial expression and increasing your hands' speed as they move.

SUN/SUNNY

CLOUDY

>> Form cloud-like bumps with alternating hands. Make sure NOT to move both hands simultaneously.

WIND

>> Modify your facial expression depending on how windy it is.

RAIN

>> Modify your facial expression depending on how rainy it is.

SNOW

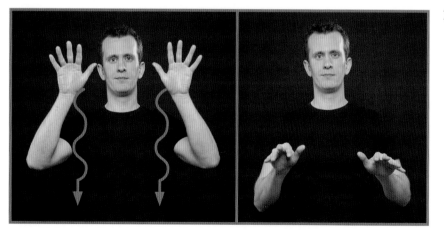

>> Flick fingers in a downward motion slowly. Modify your facial expression depending on how much it is snowing.

plants

TREE

>> Twist your
wrist twice.

Possible Classifier Example >> TREE

Trees

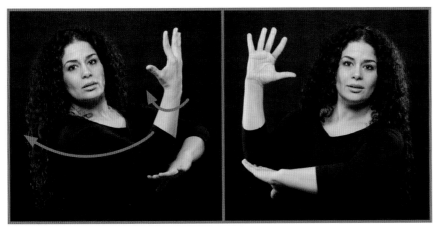

>> Modify this
sign by signing
toward where the
trees are and/or
emphasizing your
facial expression
according to how
many trees there
are or how thick
the trees are.

LEAVES

>> Move your hand like a falling leaf.

BUSHES

>> Modify your facial expression depending on the size of the bushes, and sign toward the location of the bushes if desired.

GRASS

2x

GROW

>> Repeat in a slightly different location to sign "Garden." Sign once for "Growing."

FLOWERS

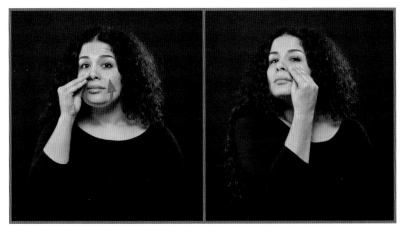

animals

ANIMAL

>> Move your hands toward each other while keeping your fingers on your chest. Repeat. For more animal signs, see the Home >> Pets section (on page 85).

FARM

HORSE

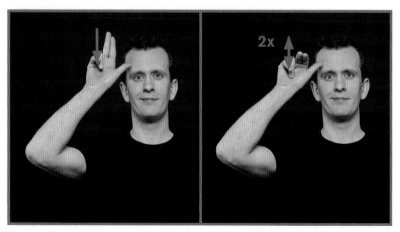

COW

>> Make "Y" handshapes and move your hands upward. (Note: head movement not necessary.)

PIG

FISH

DUCK

>> Flick your fingers and thumb like a duck's beak.

BEAR

MONKEY

ELEPHANT

>> Move hand down in an arc, like the shape of an elephant's trunk.

LION

TIGER

2x

BUG/INSECT

MOSQUITO

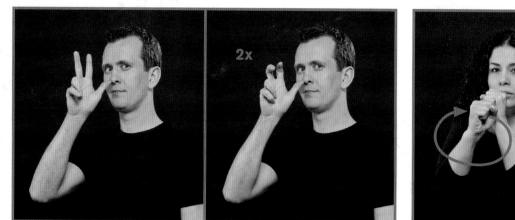

BEE

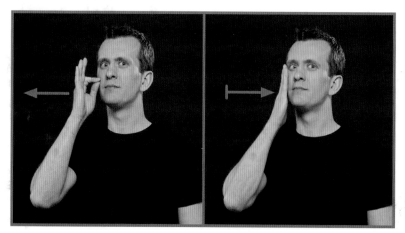

>> Make a "B" handshape
while pulling your hand
away from your face,
then change to a flat
palm and move your
hand back to your face.

BEE OR BIRD FLYING

>> Make a "1" handshape
and move your hand like
it's flying. Make sure to
make a flying face!

>> VERBS

general

ARRIVE

>> Sign in the
direction
of arrival.

LEAVE

>> Sign in the
direction of
the exit.

STAY

>> Sign once for "Stay."
Repeat to sign "Staying."

KEEP

>> Bring your dominant
hand down to your other
hand, with both in a
"K" handshape. Modify
this sign by signing toward
what you're referring to.

TAKE

>> Modify this sign
by signing toward
the person who
is taking.

GIVE

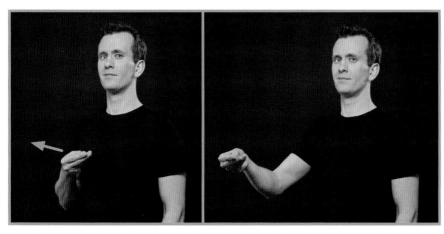

>> Modify this sign by signing toward the person you are giving to.

Possible Classifier Example >> GIVE

Give the Gift

>> Sign toward the person you're giving the gift to. Modify your handshapes depending on the shape and size of the gift, and modify your facial expression to show the weight of the gift.

GIVE TO ME

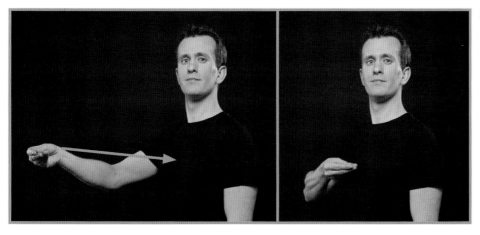

>> Sign away from the person who is giving.

LOOK/WATCH

>> Sign toward what you're looking at and move your head to the left and right repeatedly.

MAKE

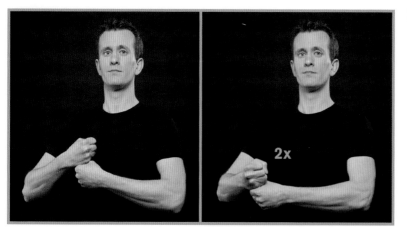

>> Twist hands in opposite directions. Repeat for "Make." Repeat continuously to sign "Making."

SHOW YOU

>> With your dominant index finger in the middle of your non-dominant palm, move both hands together toward the person you're showing.

SHOW ME

>> With your dominant index finger in the middle of your non-dominant palm, move both hands together away from the person who is showing.

IGNORE

>> Sign toward what you are ignoring.

communication

SPEAK

TELL

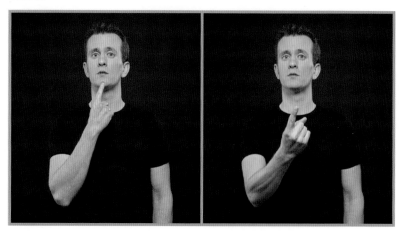

>> Sign toward the person you're telling.

ASK HIM/HER/THEM

>> Sign toward the person you're asking.

ASK ME

>> Sign away from the person who is asking.

ACCEPT

>> Sign once. To sign "Passive," repeat and add a passive facial expression.

REJECT

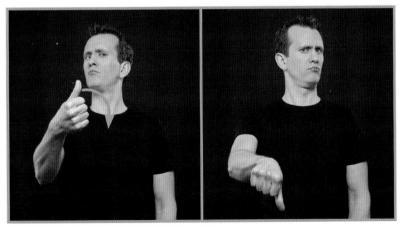

>> Make sure to emphasize your facial expression. Shake your head if desired.

AGREE

>> Sign toward the person you're agreeing with. Make sure to emphasize your facial expression and nod while signing.

DISAGREE

>> Make sure to emphasize your facial expression.

household

SLEEP

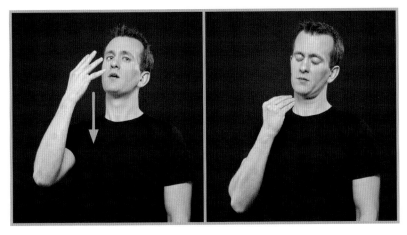

>> Make sure to emphasize your facial expression.

WAKE UP

>> Make sure to emphasize your facial expression.

CARRY HERE

>> Sign toward where you're carrying.

CARRY THERE

>> Sign toward where you're carrying.

Possible Classifier Example >> CARRY THERE

Carry the Bag There

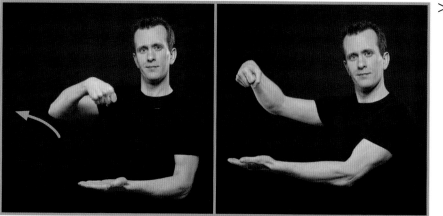

>> Sign toward where you're carrying. Modify this sign by showing the size or shape of the bag with your handshape, and/or showing the weight of the bag with your facial expression.

BRING HERE

>> Sign toward where you're bringing.

Possible Classifier Example >> BRING HERE

Bring the Box Here

>> Modify this sign by changing your handshape based on the box's shape and size.

BRING THERE

>> Sign toward where you're bringing.

Possible Classifier Example >> BRING THERE

Bring the Cup There

>> Sign toward where you're bringing and modify your handshape depending on the size of the cup.

PICK UP

>> Sign toward where you're picking the object up.

PUT DOWN/LEAVE IT

>> Sign toward what you're referring to.

CLEAN UP

>> Sign toward where you're cleaning up.

PUT AWAY

>> Sign toward where you're putting away.

Possible Classifier Example >> PUT AWAY

Put the Books on the Shelves

2x

>> Make sure to sign "book" twice. Sign toward where books are being put away, and modify your hand-shape according to the size or shape of the book.

CHANGE

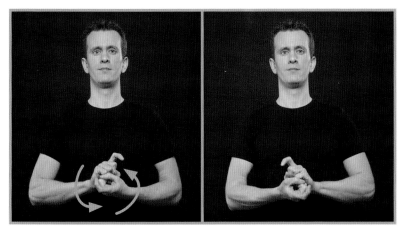

THROW AWAY

>> Sign toward what you're referring to.

action

SIT

>> Make sure not to confuse with the sign for "Chair" by signing only once.

GO THERE

>> Sign toward where "there" is.

COME HERE

>> Sign toward where "here" is.

MOVE THERE

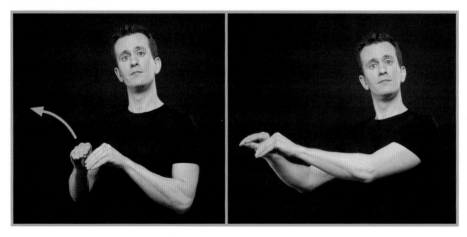

>> Sign toward where "there" is.

MOVE HERE

>> Sign toward where "here" is.

JUMP

Possible Classifier Example >> JUMP

Jump Down onto the Floor

>> Sign in the direction of jumping. Make sure to emphasize your facial expression to show how far the person jumped.

CLIMB

>> Repeat for "Climb."
Repeat continuously
to sign "Climbing."

TWIRL

HURRY

>> Make sure to emphasize
your facial expression
and sign quickly to
emphasize speed.

SLOW

>> Sign slowly.

DESCRIPTORS

general

SAME

>> Sign toward what you're referring to.

DIFFERENT

>> Make sure not to confuse this sign with "But" (page 27) by ending the sign outside your normal signing area.

FAST

>> Make sure to emphasize your facial expression. Sign once for "Fast." Repeat to sign "Faster." Sign more quickly and with a more intense facial expression for "So fast!"

SOFT

>> Make sure to emphasize your facial expression.

HARD

>> Make sure to emphasize your facial expression by showing how hard it is!

SMALL

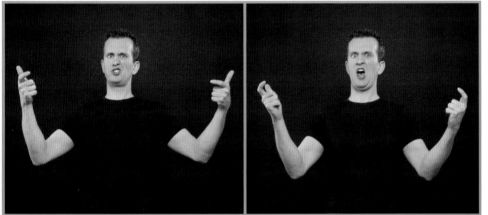

>> Make an "Ooo" facial expression as shown.

BIG

>> Use a "Cha" or "Puff" facial expression (page 8).

NEW

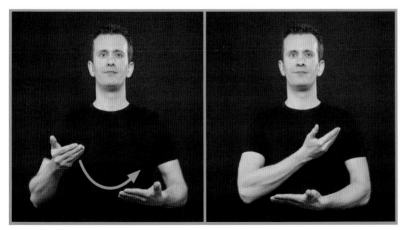

BETTER

>> Sign once for "Better." Repeat to sign "Better and better."

BEST

>> Make sure not to confuse this sign with "Better" by using an exaggerated, wider movement and emphasizing your facial expression.

WORSE/WORST

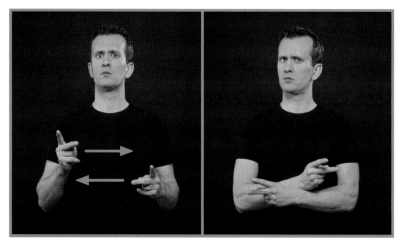

>> Make sure to emphasize your facial expression.

NEAT/CLEAN

>> Make sure not to confuse this sign with "Nice" (page 241) by repeating the sign and signing toward the location you're talking about.

DIRTY

>> Wiggle your fingers while signing. Make sure to emphasize your facial expression.

MESSY

>> Make sure to emphasize your facial expression. (Note: Wiggling your fingers is not necessary.)

STRANGE/WEIRD

>> Make sure to emphasize your facial expression.

NORMAL

IMPORTANT

>> Make sure to emphasize your facial expression.

Possible Classifier Example >> IMPORTANT

Very Important

>> Make sure to emphasize your facial expression.

colors

COLOR

>> Wiggle your fingers
while signing.

RED

BLUE

YELLOW

BLACK

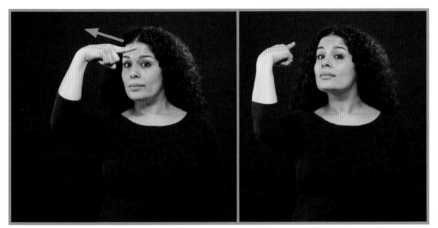

WHITE

ORANGE

>> This is also the sign for the fruit Orange.

GREEN

PURPLE

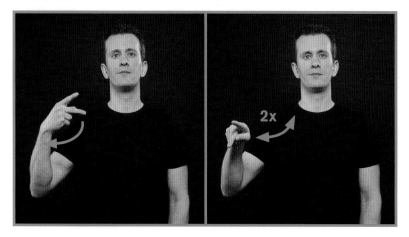

PINK

BROWN

GRAY

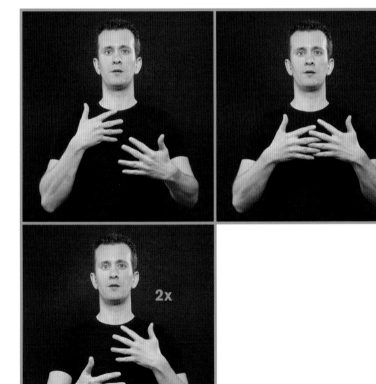

>> With fingers open wide, move one hand front-to-back while the other moves back-to-front and repeat.

BRIGHT

>> Use this non-manual signal (facial expression) while signing a color to indicate brightness.

DARK

>> Use this non-manual signal (facial expression) while signing a color to indicate dimness.

emotions

PROUD

>> Facial expressions are a vital component of signing emotions. A more intese facial expression indicates an more intense feeling.

HAPPY

SAD

ANGRY

SCARED

CONFUSED

EMBARRASSED

ANNOYED

WORRIED

>> Make sure NOT to sign with both hands simultaneously.

CRY

Make sure >> NOT to sign with both hands simultaneously.

SLEEPY

MAD

HATE

>> Flick your middle fingers and thumbs open while moving your hands down.

DETEST

EXCITED

>> Move your hands in alternating circles with your middle fingers bent.

2x

NERVOUS

>> With index fingers pointed, keep your non-dominant hand still while your dominant hand quickly shakes.

BORED

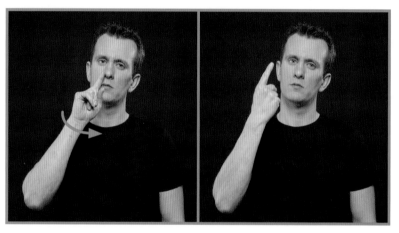

ANXIOUS

SERIOUS

SURPRISED

LAUGH

BELLY LAUGH

how many / much

TWO OF US

>> Sign toward whom
you're talking about.

THREE OF US

>> Sign toward whom
you're talking about.

FOUR OF US

>> Sign toward whom
you're talking about.
Make the handshape
for any other number
(besides 2) and
sign the same way
to signify "of us."

TWO OF THEM

>> Sign toward who or what you're talking about.

FOUR OF THEM

>> Sign toward whom or what you're talking about. Make the hand-shape for any other number (besides 2) and sign the same way to signify "of them."

LESS

MORE

FEW/SEVERAL

>> Hunch your shoulders inward and use an "Ooo" facial expression (page 8) to sign "Few." Move your shoulders wider and use a "Mmm" facial expression (page 8) for "Several."

EVERY

MANY

>> Make sure to emphasize your facial expression depending on how many.

ANY

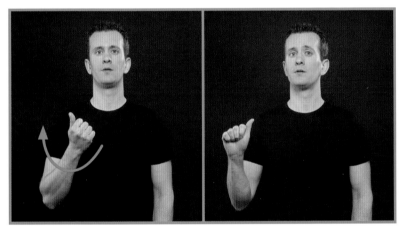

ALL

>> Move your dominant hand around your other hand (front to back) twice before coming to rest.

ALWAYS

>> Make a "1" handshape
and twirl.

NEVER

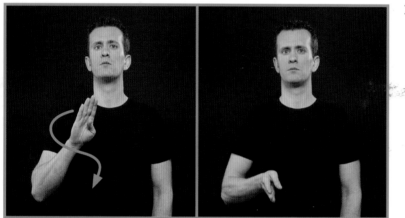

>> Make sure to emphasize
your facial expression.

SOMETIMES

people

SHORT (Height)

TALL

>> To sign "Really tall" make a "Cha" facial expression (page 8).

FUNNY

>> Wiggle your two fingers near your nose.

STUBBORN

BEARD

>> Emphasize your facial expression according to how big the beard is.

MUSTACHE

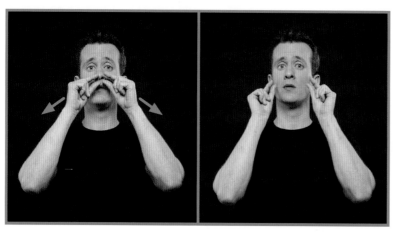

>> Make a "G" handshape or use a different hand-shape depending on the mustache's shape/style.

HAIR

Possible Classifier Examples >> HAIR

Short Hair

>> Modify this sign by signing near your shoulder or above your ear to indicate different hair lengths.

Long Hair

>> Modify this sign by signing near where the hair falls to indicate different hair lengths.

Possible Classifier Examples >> HAIR

Curly Hair

>> Modify this sign by moving your hand downward until the approximate location of where the hair ends.

Wavy Hair

>> Modify this sign by moving your hand downward until the approximate location of where the hair ends.

Straight Hair

>> Modify this sign by moving your hand downward until the approximate location of where the hair ends.

Possible Classifier Examples >> HAIR

Blonde

PIGTAILS

>> To sign "Ponytail," just use one hand and sign from the back of the head.

STUPID

SMART

>> Twist your hand while moving it up and outward.

GENIUS

>> Make sure to keep your index finger and thumb apart, then close them after you move your hand upward.

IGNORANT/CLUELESS

POOR/PITY

>> Make sure not to confuse with "Computer" (page 107) by moving your hands in the same direction as each other and emphasizing your facial expression.

NICE/KIND

>> Make sure to emphasize your facial expression.

MEAN

>> Make sure to keep your hands open until the end of the movement, and emphasize your facial expression.

ATTRACTIVE/HOT

>> Make sure to emphasize your facial expression. Sign toward the person you're referring to.

BEAUTIFUL/PRETTY/HANDSOME

>> Close your hand while moving it in a circle simultaneously. Make sure to emphasize your facial expression to show how beautiful!

Possible Classifier Examples >> BEAUTIFUL

Really Beautiful

>> Make sure to emphasize your facial expression.

UGLY

>> Make sure to emphasize your facial expression to show how ugly!

CHUBBY

>> Although it may seem extreme, this sign is commonly used in the ASL community to describe someone's girth. However, it's usually considered impolite to modify it by showing the size of the person. Instead, repeat the sign and use a "Puff" facial expression (page 8) to show greater weight.

THIN

>> Make an "Ooo" facial expression, as shown.

OLD

>> To sign "Really Old" use a "Puff" facial expression (page 8).

YOUNG

POOR (Money)

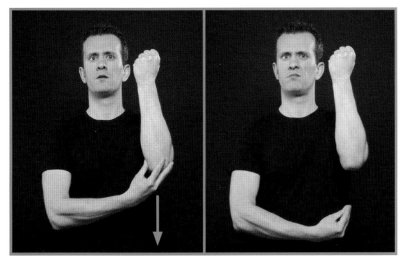

>> Make sure to emphasize your facial expression.

RICH

5 (age)

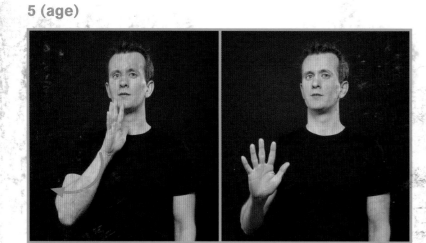

>> When signing ages, make sure to touch your index finger to your chin before signing the numeral.

25 (age)

30 (age)

when

LATE

>> Make sure to emphasize your facial expression; intensify it for "Really late."

LATER

>> Move an "L" handshape across your non-dominant palm.

EARLY

>> Make sure to emphasize your facial expression depending on how early.

NOW

>> Make sure not to confuse this sign with "Today" (page 42) by only signing once and using the proper facial expression.

SOON

>> Make an "Ooo" or a "Sss" facial expression (page 8) with this sign.

where

LOCATION

>> Sign once for "Location."
Repeat to sign "Local."

NEAR/CLOSE BY

>> Use a "Sss" facial
expression (page 8)
to sign "Really Close."

FAR

>> Sign in a wider area
to show how far. Use
a "Puff" or "Cha"
facial expression
(page 8).

ABOVE

BELOW

LOW

>> Make sure not to confuse this sign with "Short" (page 235) by using the proper facial expression.

HIGH

>> Sign higher to show how high. Use a "Puff" or "Cha" facial expression (page 8).

INDEX

RESOURCES

Books

Inside Deaf Culture, Carol Padden and Tom Humphries. Harvard University Press: 2006.

An in-depth examination of Deaf culture, including the history of ASL and the Deaf community and how its culture has changed since the early era of the language.

The Deaf Mute Howls, Albert Ballin. Gallaudet University Press: 1998 (reprint edition).

One of the first books ever written by a Deaf person, this book from the 1930s went against the tradition of teaching Deaf children to speak and read lips, and advocated for teaching sign language to both Deaf and hearing people alike.

Deaf Again, Mark Drolsbaug. Handwave Publications, 2008.

A unique autobiography that explores the meaning of being "culturally Deaf," written by a hard-of-hearing, then Deaf man who searches to find his place in the Deaf community.

Hands of My Father: A Hearing Boy, His Deaf Parents, and the Language of Love, Myron Uhlberg. Bantam: 2009.

A memoir by a CODA (child of a deaf adult) about his hearing perspective while growing up in the Deaf community of 1940s Brooklyn.

A Loss for Words: The Story of Deafness in a Family, Lou Ann Walker. Harper Perennial: 1987.

A moving story of a CODA growing up with Deaf parents in the Midwest in the 1950s.

Websites

NAD.org

The official website of the National Association of the Deaf, the premier civil rights organization of, by, and for deaf and hard-of-hearing individuals in the US.

DeafNation.com

The go-to site for videos and news for the Deaf and hard-of-hearing community, as well as information about their popular DeafNation Expos around the US and world.

WFDeaf.org

The website of the World Federation of the Deaf (WFD), an international organization of Deaf people that represents their needs and interests worldwide, with a focus on developing nations.

YouTube.com

YouTube is a great place to practice your ASL and learn more about the Deaf community. To find ASL videos on YouTube, simply type in keywords like "Deaf," "ASL," "ASL poetry," or "ASL music." Be aware, however, that like most online videos, some are much more authoritative than others. While many videos are made by Deaf people themselves, others are made by children of deaf parents (CODA), those who learned ASL through classes, or those with a tertiary understanding of the language. Similarly, many movies featuring Deaf people often have issues with ASL translation, actors with a poor understanding of ASL, or are shot in a way that makes it hard to see what's being signed.

ACKNOWLEDGMENTS

Models Shelly Guy and Garret Zuercher helped us produce the wonderful photos for this book, along with photographer Mark Gore and assistant Daniel Stasser. Their hard work and input was much appreciated! Thank you to Quarto Publishing, especially Michelle Faulkner and Jeffrey McLaughlin, for embracing an all-inclusive ASL book; Jennifer Boudinot for bringing it all together; and Lynne Yeamans for her impactful design. Finally, special thanks to Russell Rosen for his indispensible guidance and expertise.